Dear Isabel,
Happy 14th Birthday.
Love The SACKS
11/02

*To accomplish great things,
we must not only act,
but also dream,
not only plan,
but also believe.*

— Anatole France

Other books in this series…

Blue Mountain Arts®

A Friend Lives in Your Heart Forever

A Mother Is Love

I Love You Soooo Much
by Douglas Pagels

I'd Love to Give These Gifts to You

Sister, You Have a Special Place in My Heart

The Greatest Gift of All Is… A Daughter like You

The Greatest Gift of All Is… A Son like You

Keep Believing in Yourself

and Your Special

Dreams

*Words to Motivate & Inspire
Your Dreams*

SPS Studios™

Boulder, Colorado

Library of Congress Catalog Card Number: 2001005732
ISBN: 0-88396-614-X

We wish to thank Susan Polis Schutz for permission to reprint the following poems that appear in this publication: "You Deserve a Life of Happiness" and "Always Create Your Own Dreams and Live Life to the Fullest." Copyright © 1983, 1989 by Stephen Schutz and Susan Polis Schutz. And for "Know Yourself." Copyright © 1997 by Susan Polis Schutz. All rights reserved.

ACKNOWLEDGMENTS appear on page 48.

Certain trademarks are used under license.

Manufactured in Thailand
First Printing: January 2002

 This book is printed on recycled paper.

Library of Congress Cataloging-in-Publication Data

Keep believing in yourself and your special dreams : words to motivate and inspire your dreams.
    p. cm.
  ISBN 0-88396-614-X (hardcover : alk. paper)
  1. Success—Quotations, maxims, etc. 2. Conduct of life—Quotations, maxims, etc.
I. SPS Studios.
  PN6084.S78 K44 2002
  158.1—dc21

                                                                    2001005732
                                                                    CIP

SPS Studios, Inc.
P.O. Box 4549, Boulder, Colorado 80306

Contents

(Authors listed in order of first appearance)

Always Believe in Yourself and Your Dreams

As you go on in this world, keep looking forward to the future... to all you might be.

Don't let old mistakes or misfortunes hold you down: learn from them, forgive yourself — or others — and move on. Do not be bothered or discouraged by adversity. Instead, meet it as a challenge. Be empowered by the courage it takes you to overcome obstacles. Learn things. Learn something new every day.

Be interested in others and what they might teach you. But do not look for yourself in the faces of others. Do not look for who you are in other people's approval. As far as who you are and who you will become goes — the answer is always within yourself. Believe in yourself. Follow your heart and your dreams. You — like everyone else — will make mistakes. But as long as you are true to the strength within your own heart... you can never go wrong.

— Ashley Rice

Believe in All That You Are

As the dawn of each morning
peers into your life,
there lies a path to follow.
Delicate whispers can be heard
if you listen to the sound of your heart
and the voice that speaks within you.

If you listen closely to your soul,
you will become aware of your dreams
that are yet to unfold.
You will discover that there lies within you
a voice of confidence and strength
that will prompt you to seek a journey
and live a dream.

Within the depths of your mind,
the purpose and direction of your life
can be determined by listening intently
to the knowledge that you already possess.
Your heart, mind, and soul
are the foundation
of your success and happiness.

In the still of each passing moment,
may you come to understand that
you are capable of reaching a higher destiny.
When you come to believe in all that you are
and all that you can become,
there will be no cause for doubt.
Believe in your heart, for it offers hope.
Believe in your mind, for it offers direction.
Believe in your soul, for it offers strength.
But above all else... believe in yourself.

— Leslie Neilson

Ten Important Traveling Companions to Take with You on the Journey to Your Dreams

1. **Confidence:** for when things get tough, when you're overwhelmed, when you think of giving up

2. **Patience:** with your own trials and temptations, and with others

3. **An adjustable attitude:** one that doesn't react, but responds with well-thought-out actions and feelings

4. **Beauty:** within yourself, in your surroundings, and in nature

5. **Excitement:** new things to enjoy and learn and experience

6. **Fun:** laughter and smiles any way you can get them

7. **Companionship:** people to share your happiness and sorrows, your troubles and joys

8. **Health:** mental, physical, and emotional

9. **Peace:** with others, yourself, and in your environment

10. **Love:** pure, unconditional, and eternal

— Barbara Cage

Don't Be Afraid to Dream Big

Let nothing hold you back from exploring
  your wildest fantasies, wishes, and aspirations.
Don't be afraid to dream big
and to follow your dreams wherever they lead you.
Open your eyes to their beauty;
open your mind to their magic;
open your heart to their possibilities.
Only by dreaming will you ever discover
who you are, what you want, and what you can do.
Don't be afraid to take risks, to become involved,
  to make a commitment.
Do whatever it takes to make
  your dreams come true.
Always believe in miracles,
  and always believe in you!

— Julie Anne Ford

Don't put limits on yourself.
So many dreams are waiting to be realized.
Decisions are too important to leave to chance.
Reach for your peak, your goal, your prize.

Realize that it's never too late.
Do ordinary things in an extraordinary way.
Have health and hope and happiness.
Take the time to wish upon a star.

— Collin McCarty

Whatever you can do,
or dream you can... begin it.
Boldness has genius, power
and magic in it.

— Johann Wolfgang von Goethe

Believe in Miracles!

Love your life.
Believe in your own power,
   your potential,
      and your innate goodness.
Every morning, wake with the awe
   of just being alive.
Each day, discover the magnificent,
   awesome beauty in the world.
Explore and embrace life in yourself
   and in everyone you see each day.
Reach within to find your own specialness.
Amaze yourself,
   and rouse those around you
      to the potential of each new day.

Don't be afraid to admit
that you are less than perfect;
this is the essence of your humanity.
Let those who love you help you.
Trust enough to be able to take.
Look with hope to the horizon of today,
for today is all we truly have.
Live this day well.
Let a little sunshine out as well as in.
Create your own rainbows.
Be open to all your possibilities;
possibilities can be miracles.
Always believe in miracles!

— Vickie M. Worsham

You Deserve
a Life of Happiness

You will get only what you seek
Choose your goals carefully
Know what you like
and what you do not like
Be critical about what you can do well
and what you cannot do well
Choose a career or lifestyle that interests you
and work hard to make it a success
but also have fun in what you do
Be honest with people
    and help them if you can
but don't depend on anyone
    to make life easy or happy for you
(only you can do that for yourself)

Be strong and decisive
but remain sensitive
Regard your family, and the idea of family
as the basis for security, support and love
Understand who you are
and what you want in life
before sharing your life with someone
When you are ready to enter a relationship
make sure that the person is worthy of
everything you are physically and mentally
Strive to achieve your dreams
Find happiness in everything you do
Love with your entire being
Love with an uninhibited soul
Make a triumph
of every aspect
of your life

— Susan Polis Schutz

It's Up to You

This life is the only one
you're given.
Look for opportunities to grow,
and never be discouraged
in your efforts to do so.
Replace your weaknesses
with positives;
take life's broken pieces
and re-create your dreams.
Never measure the future
by the past;
let yesterday become a memory
and tomorrow a promise.

Begin each day by focusing
on all that is good,
and you'll be in a position
to handle whatever comes along.
Take responsibility for
your actions;
never make excuses
for not being the best
you can be.
If you should slip,
be comforted by the thought
that we all do at times.
Determine your tomorrows
by the choices you make today,
and you'll find yourself living
in joy and triumph.

— Linda E. Knight

If Ever You Feel Discouraged...

Hang in there and have patience with yourself and the situation.
Live in the moment, one day at a time,
not fretting about the past or worrying about the future.
Don't take on more than you have to; learn to let go.
Refuse negative thoughts; replace them with positive ones.
Look for the good things in your life
and make a point of appreciating them.
Believe in yourself and know
that you have the power to do anything.
You are ultimately the one in charge of your life
and the only person in the world who can change it.
No matter how much others are pulling for you
or how much anyone else cares,
<u>you</u> must do what needs to be done
to make your present and future
everything you want it to be.

— Barbara Cage

Never Give Up Hope

Hope is knowing that there are wonderful possibilities
    and that miracles can happen.
Hope is believing that until nothing is left,
    something good exists somewhere.
Hope is understanding that change is possible
    and that anything can happen.
Hope is being able to imagine that something positive
    can eventually come out of heartache and pain
    and that nothing and no one is hopeless.
Hope gives each of us the courage to face life's challenges,
    the motivation to move forward,
    and the strength to go on.

— Barbara Cage

Believe... and Your Dreams Will Take You There

Trust in yourself, and you will find
beautiful things awaiting you.
Have faith in yourself.
As long as you remain strong,
you will find the light that makes
the star within your heart glisten.
Look to the morals that have always brought you strength.
Find encouragement in each step you take,
and follow your path to the most joyful endings.
Let your heart be open to the warmth and compassion
that others have to offer you.
Great potential lies within you.
You hold your own destiny in your hand
and your aspirations in your heart.
You have so many places that you can go.
Believe... and your dreams will take you there.

— Shannon M. Lester

Twelve Ways to Keep Smiling!

Hold on to your dreams, and never let them go ✣
Show the rest of the world how wonderful you are! ✣
Give circumstances a chance, and give others the
benefit of the doubt ✣ Wish on a star that shines in
your sky ✣ Take on your problems one by one and
work things out ✣ Rely on all the strength you have
inside ✣ Let loose the sparkle and spirit that you
sometimes try to hide ✣ Stay in touch with those who
touch your life with love ✣ Look on the bright side
and don't let adversity keep you from winning ✣ Be
yourself, because you are filled with special qualities
that have brought you this far and that will always see
you through ✣ Keep your spirits up ✣ Make your
heart happy, and let it reflect on everything you do!

— Douglas Pagels

Be Strong,
and Don't Give Up

Remember... there is a deeper strength
and an amazing abundance of peace
available to you.
Draw from this well;
call on your faith to uphold you.
Life continues around us,
even when our troubles seem to stop time.
There is always good in life.
Take a few minutes to distract yourself
from your concerns —
long enough to draw strength from a tree
or to find pleasure in a bird's song.
Return a smile;
realize that life is a series of levels,
cycles of ups and downs —
some easy, some challenging...

Through it all, we learn;
we grow strong in faith;
we mature in understanding.
The difficult times are often the best teachers,
and there is good to be found in all situations.
Reach for the good.
Be strong, and don't give up.

— Pamela Owens Renfro

*W*hat lies behind us
and what lies before us
are tiny matters
compared to what lies within us.

— Ralph Waldo Emerson

This is how it works.

Each new day is a blank page in the diary of
your life. The pen is in your hand, but the lines
will not all be written the way you choose; some
will come from the world and the circumstances
that surround you. But for the many things that
<u>are</u> in your control, there is something special
you need to know...

The secret of life is in making your story as
beautiful as it can be. Write the diary of your
days and fill the pages with words that come
from the heart. As the pages take you through
time, you will discover paths that will add to
your happiness and your sorrows, but if you can
do these things, there will always be hope in
your tomorrows.

Follow your dreams. Work hard. Be kind. This is all anyone could ever ask: Do what you can to make the door open on a day... that is filled with beauty in some special way. Remember: Goodness will be rewarded. Smiles will pay you back. Have fun. Find strength. Be truthful. Have faith. Don't focus on the things you lack.

Realize that people are the treasures in life — and happiness is the real wealth. Have a diary that describes how you did your best, and...

The rest will take care of itself.

— Douglas Pagels

Know Yourself

Know what you can
and want to do in life
Set goals for yourself
and work hard to achieve them
Strive to have fun every day
Use your creativity as a means
of expressing your feelings
Be sensitive in viewing the world
Develop a sense of confidence
Be honest with yourself
and with others
Follow your heart
and adhere to your own truths
Know that the more you give
the more you will receive
Believe in yourself
and your dreams will come true

— Susan Polis Schutz

$\mathcal{B}$e what you are,
and become
what you are capable
of becoming.

— Robert Louis Stevenson

$\mathcal{D}$o not wish to be anything
but what you are,
and try to be that perfectly.

— St. Francis de Sales

The Path to a Dream

The path to a dream is paved with sacrifices
and lined with determination.
And though it has many stumbling blocks
　　along the way
and may go in more than one direction,
　　it is marked with faith.
It is traveled by belief and courage,
　　persistence and hard work.
It is conquered with a willingness
to face challenges and take chances,
　　to fail and try again and again.
Along the way, you may have to confront
　　doubts, setbacks, and unfairness.
But when the path comes to an end,
you will find that there is no greater joy
than making your dream come true.

— Barbara Cage

*I*magine... Here you are, on the high peak of a mountain. You can choose to wing your way toward the clouds, or you can simply walk the usual, ordinary paths that lead to the valley below.

Which choice will you make —
the well-worn paths or rising above it all?

Beautiful things await you
if you can reach the heights.

— George Sand

*D*o not follow where
the path may lead.
*G*o, instead, where there is no path
and leave a trail.

— Anonymous

When the task at hand is a mountain in front of you...

It may seem too hard to climb.
But you don't have to climb it
all at once —
just one step at a time.
Take one small step...
and one small step...
then another...
and you'll find...
the task at hand that was a mountain
in front of you...

...is a mountain
you have climbed.

— Ashley Rice

You've Got to Keep On!

It is said that once you stop striving,
You start falling.
Don't fall.
You are a wondrous human package
Of achievement, talent, and potential,
So keep on...

Climb that mountain,
Dream that dream,
Live that vision,
Follow that quest.
Whatever it takes,
Whatever goals you pursue,
Keep on!

— Susan A. J. Lyttek

Anything Is Possible!

Believe in what makes you feel good.
Believe in what makes you happy.
Believe in the dreams you've always wanted
    to come true, and give them every chance to.
Life holds no promises as to what will come your way.
You must search for your own ideals
    and work toward reaching them.
Life makes no guarantees as to what you'll have.
It just gives you time to make choices
    and to take chances
and to discover whatever secrets might come your way.
If you are willing to take
    the opportunities you are given
        and utilize the abilities you have,
you will constantly fill your life with
    special moments and unforgettable times...

No one knows the mysteries of life
    or its ultimate meaning,
but for those who are willing to believe
    in their dreams and in themselves,
life is a precious gift
    in which anything is possible.

— Dena Dilaconi

To accomplish great things,
we must not only act,
but also dream,
not only plan,
but also believe.

— Anatole France

Share Your Dreams with Others

Surround yourself with
those who believe in you
and who will help you achieve
your goals.

— Lisa Marie Yost

If people offer
their help or wisdom
as you go through life,
accept it gratefully.
You can learn much from those
who have gone before you.

— Edmund O'Neill

The Dream Box

I collected dreams for a while
And stored them in a little box
On my windowsill
Some were as polished as baby pearls
Others as jagged as pieces of uncut jade
Like raw stones
They tumbled in my mind
Some for days, others for years
I guarded them like tiny treasures
Keeping them for myself
Until one day I opened the box
To tinker with them
And they were gone
Like wandering children
I had not understood…
They were on loan and must be shared
Or lost forever

— Parvene Michaels

Keep Believing
in a Better Tomorrow

Sometimes it gets so hard to focus on what's really important in our lives. We tend to let the petty, everyday nonsense blur the view of our tomorrows.

Sometimes our hearts misplace the passion for our dreams, and doubt seems to take over all our plans — compromising the future we long to see. These emotions that confuse us or set us back are not signs of weakness; they are signs of our humanity, and accepting their existence is a strength we all can call upon.

If we allow ourselves to step back, we can take a moment to look at where we were and how far we've come. We're the ones who must choose either to dwell on bitter endings or use the painful knowledge to move on.

We must keep on believing, keep on fighting, and never forget who we are and what we're working toward.

— Michele Lee

...and Remember to Live Life One Day at a Time

*O*ur lives are made up of a million moments, spent in a million different ways. Some are spent searching for love, peace, and harmony. Others are spent surviving day to day. But there is no greater moment than when we discover the most wonderful truth of all: we have it within our power to be fully satisfied and live a life with true meaning.

One day at a time — we have that ability, through cherishing each moment and rejoicing in each dream. We can experience each day anew, and with this fresh start we have what it takes to make all our dreams come true. Each day is new, and living one day at a time enables us to truly enjoy life and live it to the fullest.

— Regina Hill

Always Create Your Own Dreams and Live Life to the Fullest

Dreams can come true
if you take the time to
think about what you want in life
Get to know yourself
Find out who you are
Choose your goals carefully
Be honest with yourself
Always believe in yourself
Find many interests and pursue them
Find out what is important to you
Find out what you are good at
Don't be afraid to make mistakes
Work hard to achieve successes

When things are not going right
don't give up — just try harder
Give yourself freedom to try out new things
Laugh and have a good time
Open yourself up to love
Take part in the beauty of nature
Be appreciative of all that you have
Help those less fortunate than you
Work towards peace in the world
Live life to the fullest
Create your own dreams and
follow them until they are a reality

— Susan Polis Schutz

Don't Ever Forget that You Are Special

Don't ever forget that you are unique.
Be your best self
and not an imitation of someone else.
Find your strengths
and use them in a positive way.
Don't listen to those
who ridicule the choices you make.
Travel the road that you have chosen
and don't look back with regret.
You have to take chances
to make your dreams happen.
Remember that there is plenty of time
to travel another road — and still another —
in your journey through life.
Take the time to find the route
that is right for you.

You will learn something valuable
from every trip you take,
so don't be afraid to make mistakes.
Tell yourself that you're okay
just the way you are.
Make friends who respect your true self.
Take the time to be alone, too,
so you can know just how terrific
your own company can be.
Remember that being alone
doesn't always mean being lonely;
it can be a beautiful experience
of finding your creativity,
your heartfelt feelings,
and the calm and quiet peace deep inside you.
Don't ever forget that you are special.

— Jacqueline Schiff

Follow Your Destiny, Wherever It Leads You

There comes a time in your life when you realize that if you stand still, you will remain at this point forever. You realize that if you fall and stay down, life will pass you by.

Life's circumstances are not always what you might wish them to be. The pattern of life does not necessarily go as you plan. Beyond any understanding, you may at times be led in different directions that you never imagined, dreamed, or designed. Yet if you had never put any effort into choosing a path, or tried to carry out your dream, then perhaps you would have no direction at all.

Rather than wondering about or questioning the direction your life has taken, accept the fact that there is a path before you now. Shake off the "why's" and "what if's," and rid yourself of confusion. Whatever was — is in the past. Whatever is — is what's important. The past is a brief reflection. The future is yet to be realized. Today is here.

Walk your path one step at a time — with courage, faith, and determination. Keep your head up, and cast your dreams to the stars. Soon your steps will become firm and your footing will be solid again. A path that you never imagined will become the most comfortable direction you could have ever hoped to follow.

Keep your belief in yourself and walk into your new journey. You will find it magnificent, spectacular, and beyond your wildest imaginings.

— Vicki Silvers

Keep Believing in Yourself
and Your Special Dreams

There may be days when
you get up in the morning and
things aren't the way you had hoped they would be.
That's when you have to
tell yourself that things will get better.
There will be times when people
disappoint you and let you down,
but those are the times when you must remind yourself
to trust your own judgments and opinions,
to keep your life focused on believing in yourself
and all that you are capable of.
There will be challenges to face
and changes to make in your life,
and it is up to you to accept them.
Constantly keep yourself headed
in the right direction for you.

It may not be easy at times,
but in those times of struggle
you will find a stronger sense of who you are,
and you will see yourself developing
into the person you have always wanted to be.

Life is a journey through time,
filled with many choices;
each of us will experience life in our own special way.
So when the days come that are filled
with frustration and unexpected responsibilities,
remember to believe in yourself
and all you want your life to be,
because the challenges and changes
will only help you to find the dreams
that you know are meant to come true for you.

— Deanna Beisser

ACKNOWLEDGMENTS

The following is a partial list of authors whom the publisher especially wishes to thank for permission to reprint their works.

Barbara Cage for "Never Give Up Hope." Copyright © 2002 by Barbara Cage. All rights reserved.

Shannon M. Lester for "Believe… and Your Dreams Will Take You There." Copyright © 2002 by Shannon M. Lester. All rights reserved.

Susan A. J. Lyttek for "You've Got to Keep On!" Copyright © 2002 by Susan A. J. Lyttek. All rights reserved.

Parvene Michaels for "The Dream Box." Copyright © 2002 by Parvene Michaels. All rights reserved.

Michele Lee for "Keep Believing in a Better Tomorrow." Copyright © 2002 by Michele Lee. All rights reserved.

A careful effort has been made to trace the ownership of poems used in this anthology in order to obtain permission to reprint copyrighted materials and give proper credit to the copyright owners. If any error or omission has occurred, it is completely inadvertent, and we would like to make corrections in future editions provided that written notification is made to the publisher:

SPS STUDIOS, INC., P.O. Box 4549, Boulder, Colorado 80306.